A Voice
of One's Own

Published in 2023 by The School of Life
First published in the USA in 2023
This paperback edition published in 2024
930 High Road, London, N12 9RT
Copyright © The School of Life 2023

Photography by Sarah Burton
Designed by Sarah Boris
Printed in Latvia by Livonia

A proportion of this book has appeared online at
www.theschooloflife.com/articles

The School of Life publishes a range of books on
essential topics in psychological and emotional
life, including relationships, parenting, friendship,
careers and fulfilment. The aim is always to help
us to understand ourselves better – and thereby to
grow calmer, less confused and more purposeful.
Discover our full range of titles, including books
for children, here:
www.theschooloflife.com/books

The School of Life also offers a comprehensive
therapy service, which complements, and draws
upon, our published works:
www.theschooloflife.com/therapy

ISBN 978-1-916753-10-5

10 9 8 7 6 5 4 3 2 1

A Voice
of One's Own

A
story about
confidence and
self-belief

The
Background

Anna wasn't, by nature, someone who liked to make a big deal of such things; the topic seemed essentially trivial and ridiculous to her. She knew what an inconsequential person she was – and how many more serious and important matters there were in the world. (She would have been surprised and appalled to know we were even thinking about her.) Still, nor could she entirely overlook – or stop covertly ruminating about – the uncomfortable detail that she would, at some point in the early hours of the following day, be turning twenty-nine.

It wasn't age itself that was the problem; it was where she stood in relation to its expectations. Twenty-nine might be very young to be prime minister or a Nobel laureate, but was it right that a twenty-nine-year-old should still not have finished her degree, still not know what she wanted in love, still feel sick whenever she had to impress anyone at work, still be regretting certain choices she had made a decade before, still regularly develop acne and still long like a pitiful infant for her mother's approval? There could, felt Anna, be few twenty-nine-year-olds more backward – and despicable – than she was.

Anna wore her self-loathing lightly. Often, extraordinarily, she was mistaken for cheerful. She tried hard to put others at ease, to agree with whatever was being said – and to disappear inoffensively into the background. Only a few people had ever really cottoned on. The anonymous stranger on the emergency helpline that she had called late one night, a clever, sensitive boy at university who had guessed at her complexities and whom she had pushed away with a sharpness she now regretted. Anna worked hard to minimise the chances of anyone feeling sorry for her – or indeed knowing her.

After dropping out of her course (her parents called this 'the incident'), Anna had taken a job in advertising. She loathed it, but without any qualifications, she had been in no position to be picky – the opportunity had come through a friend of a friend. She spent her days working on radio campaigns, usually for clients in insurance or fast food. She filled out invoices, coordinated meetings and, latterly, helped to generate ideas. Yet what she really wanted to do, if only she could feel strong enough, was to hand in her notice and finish off her remaining two years at the Royal Veterinary College, and then join a small practice, ideally in the country, looking after horses and dogs. Anna found animals every bit as reassuring and familiar as she found humans daunting and unpredictable.

Anna's mother accused her of attention-seeking. She alleged that she was forever cooking up new ways to make a fuss. First there'd been the childhood eczema, then the difficulties with her friends at school, then her sleeping problems, then the abrupt departure from university – one thing after another. 'Really, what now?' seemed to be the exasperated tone the mother adopted in relation to any problem her daughter shared with her – a habit of disclosure Anna nevertheless found hard to break. She felt ashamed. She longed to make her mother proud. She wished she wasn't such a burden. She would have liked to hide in a small box and shut the lid.

Anna rented a studio flat in a large run-down tenement block. She preferred a modest place she could call her own to sharing with friends. She found it hard to retain her balance when she was around other people too long. She needed many hours to process seemingly ordinary events; things didn't wash over her. A vast and hideous shopping centre was being built opposite; there could be drilling all day. If you missed paying your taxes, or went even a little over the speeding limit the law would come after you, but you could put up something like this and apparently break no rules.

If ever anyone wanted to destroy Anna, all they needed to do was read her diary. It was a repository of her bleakest, most confused and – in her view – silliest moods. She'd been keeping one since she was sixteen and was sure that she sounded no more mature now than she had done then. Still, she knew how much clearer her head could be once she had written a few pages. Without the slightest literary ambition, Anna was in the true sense a writer: someone who feels better after they have put pen to paper for a while.

As often happened when her spirits were low, Anna's self-hatred directed itself towards her looks. She remembered a particularly horrifying glimpse in the mirror at work: the dazed eyes, swollen cheeks and flaky skin. She worried she was ageing more rapidly than ever; she might soon be mistaken for forty. When these sorts of arguments swirled through her mind, logic or reassurance were of no use. It really didn't matter what she actually looked like; there were self-lacerating feelings that needed to find a home and they could always be sure of a welcoming one around the issue of her appearance.

When she was down, Anna was in the habit of dialling her mother. It was a peculiar idea from many angles, chiefly because of the number of times she had done so and been left feeling abandoned and humiliated. Then again, we do many things not because they necessarily make sense or render us happy, but primarily because they feel familiar.

In a vague way, Anna wanted to ask her mother if she deserved to exist, if she was OK, if she could have permission to carry on. It wasn't wholly rational, which was why Anna never quite expressed herself directly. Nevertheless, she felt that her neediness was only too easy to guess at – and to be revolted by.

When Anna mentioned that the prospect of her birthday was making her feel very old, her mother returned to a favourite theme – her daughter's lack of perspective and ingratitude. 'You should try reaching sixty! And a neighbour is turning ninety this year.' Then came another suggestion: if Anna was feeling so much pity for herself, she might try volunteering in a shelter for the homeless or an immigration centre. That would soon cure her of any angst about a birthday. Anna thanked her mother wanly, hung up, and stared blankly out of the window for an age.

There had, along the way, been a mention of a 'present'. This was in reality an invitation to travel up to Essex – two hours each way – at the weekend in order to have lunch with her parents in a pub they frequented near the family house. Once people tell us they love us and we believe them, we may end up doing the strangest, most counter-intuitive things for them.

The voices of people who were once outside us become the voices in our own minds: *You have nothing to complain about. You had a good childhood. Your father and I gave you everything you needed. You always had things ahead of other children. We loved you a lot. You've only got yourself to blame.* The way we view and address ourselves is soaked in the assessments of our earliest caregivers.

Anna had a boyfriend called Jake, the drummer in a rock band that had had a promising start a number of years ago. He supplemented his income with work as a picture hanger and a gardener. He was handsome, confident and had a ready ease with strangers. At the start, she'd been very surprised that he should have taken an interest in her – and she still often wondered what he saw in her. He was frequently away and it was at many points unclear quite why, or where. 'Supper tomorrow, 7 p.m. It's on me babe.' He could be very sweet when he remembered her.

We get thrown into profound muddles by the perplexing messages that others send us: *I love you so much;* by people who are not entirely kind. *I desire you a lot;* by people who won't have sex with us. *You should feel grateful;* by people who don't fulfil our needs. Purely difficult people are an easy proposition to spot and to handle; the really troubling ones are those who tell us they love us and then go on to inflict a sequence of covertly frustrating and painful things on us. They do something worse than hurt us, they damage our ability to think logically about what has happened.

Anna had often heard it said that one ends up attracted to people who are like one's parent(s). There was, ostensibly, very little danger of that in her case. Jake was sharply different to both her mother and father. He came from a more prosperous background. They despised his music. He wasn't the sort to take a holiday on a canal boat. But despite the many differences, in a key respect, he was strikingly akin to Anna's mother. The similarity was not so much in what they were like, but in how they made her feel. He was an expert at leaving her craving reassurance – and wondering what she might have done wrong.

Recently at work, she had been hounded by a sudden desire to throw up. She experienced a mounting nausea that blurred her mind and eventually forced her to leave for the bathroom – but she never actually was sick. The chief impact of this impulse was to add a new layer of fear to her interactions and to reduce her ability to push herself forward and accept challenges; particularly because the nausea was mostly present when she was dealing with anyone or anything important. It was as though her body was perversely signalling the true danger: that she might convince someone of her worth.

The doctor could find nothing physically wrong with her, but suggested that she could have a gluten intolerance and might have a banana for breakfast and apricots at teatime. Jake preferred the idea that she was 'thinking too much'. Her mother recommended that she 'get out more'. When her boss proposed that she fly to Barcelona to represent the company at an important biannual trade show, she thanked him but blamed an unspecified family situation for her inability to do so. However satisfying it was to progress in life, in the end, Anna generally found it a good deal safer to ensure that she failed.

When Anna wasn't terrified that she might throw up, work had another challenge for her. It took her an unfeasibly long time to get down to certain tasks. It might have looked like she was being lazy, but this was harsh. She was primarily afraid. Her reluctance didn't have anything to do with not wanting to work, it had to do with a fear of failing. Not completing something was a guarantee against messing up. So long as she hadn't done anything, she couldn't do anything *wrong*. It generally took her two hours to finish a job that would technically have required only one. She was able to get down to work only when the fear of doing nothing at all finally trumped the terror of doing something badly.

At the age of eleven, Anna had been a county champion at long-distance running. Her father had been a keen athlete in his youth and had longed to have a boy that he could train in his image. Anna had sensed his longings and tried to honour them. She had made enormous efforts on the track and they had paid off. But just as there was talk of her joining a national academy, she had pulled out of athletics entirely – much to her coach's, and her father's, frustration. She couldn't even now explain why she had abruptly squandered her talents; it simply felt untenable and off the cards to be regularly picking up silver and gold medals.

Something analogous had happened on her vet course. Anna had overcome immense competition to secure a place on it. She was the first person in her family to have gone to university. Her tutors had been delighted with her and had floated the possibility of her going on to do research after her MSc. And then, at the end of her second year (in which she had come in the top three in her year), she realised in her gut that she couldn't return. She sent a curt email asking to be deferred and fled home. Her mother had always kept a keen eye out for people who didn't know their place.

Then there was love. At around the age of fifteen, boys started to notice and take an interest in Anna. They wanted to be her friend, to invite her to parties, and with luck, to kiss her. None of this had been foreseen or felt easy to cope with. Anna's response was to dress as plainly as she could, to draw no attention to herself and do her best to put off anyone who seemed enthusiastic. Her girlfriends sweetly attempted to bolster her esteem by reporting on boys who had crushes on her, but their reassurances were agonisingly off the mark. The worry wasn't so much that no one liked her, but that a few persistent and unwary people might.

To this day, Anna preferred to dress soberly. She rarely wore anything bright or patterned. Black or grey were her favourites. She felt uncomfortable in skirts. There was a beautiful dress with patterns of orange flowers in her wardrobe that she had never had the courage to put on; she wondered what had ever persuaded her to buy it. She admired well-dressed women, occasionally felt attracted to them even, but knew that she could never join their ranks. When her optician revealed she would need glasses, it felt like a relief; another reason for people to take their interest or curiosity elsewhere.

Anna often blushed. It happened principally when she felt that someone might spot her appetite or notice her claims to existence: if someone guessed that she was hungry, needed the bathroom, felt desire or craved reassurance. She blushed when she suspected that her deeper wishes could be guessed at or when her longing to be valued was on the verge of being divined by another person. She blushed because she couldn't help but be a presence in the world, while deep down convinced that she should, with greater fairness, not be here at all.

Joachim, the young man who had liked her at university, had been tender and kind in the extreme. They had started off as friends, drawn together by their course work. He was gentle, interesting and – she recognised intellectually – handsome. But the evening that he declared his feelings was excruciating. It takes a lot of self-love to forgive those who desire us. She felt instinctively revolted by him – with an intensity she couldn't understand. He was ostensibly highly eligible and yet she was impelled to run from him, and even mock and deride him. Unkindly, she told a friend that he made her skin crawl. She had broken his heart, yet he remained on her mind. She had searched his name online on several occasions lately.

The only men that Anna traditionally felt very comfortable around were those who were identifiably uninterested in her. She felt instantly at ease knowing that a man was distracted, slightly mocking, disdainful or not looking for anything very serious. The only reason she had been able to get together with Jake was that he had told her clearly early on that he wasn't seeking commitment. They had spent the first evening speaking in a succession of fake foreign accents (Dutch, German, Japanese). After making love for the first time, they had fallen into an ironic game of pretending to be two American tourists who had woken up in a bed without any idea of who the other one was. It could have been almost funny.

Her old college acquaintance, Bindisha, had already sent her three texts: a party at her place starting at nine, bring a bottle, everyone who matters will be there, don't let me down. This kind of collision between a social obligation and her real wishes was only too familiar. She had a particularly acute fear of causing offence, of being cast out, of hurting others' feelings, all of which tended to trump her instinct to remain at home. Almost invariably, she found herself staying out far later than she wanted and smiling at things that weren't funny.

Anna was a social chameleon and in her own way, without meaning ill, a liar – she went along with the drift of whatever conversation she found herself in. If this film was meant to be good, and that band popular, she nodded in assent. She agreed a lot. One needs to have been loved very firmly and authentically in order – in adulthood – to dare to say that, in fact, one wants to go to bed early, isn't in the mood for a drink and finds opera, or rap, or Tolstoy, or graffiti a bore. Anna wasn't about to signal that she did, in fact, contrary to all expectations, have a very strong and surprisingly independent character all of her own.

Anna had begun to please as a little girl in order not to set off another family crisis, in order not to antagonise a depressive father and an unpredictable, and occasionally volcanic, mother. Who was she to make things more complicated than they already were? We're taught to worry about kids who are 'bad', but perhaps the real worry should be about the future chances of the quiet ones, the demure types at the back of the class, smiling weakly in the school photo, who always hand in their homework on time and cause no trouble at all.

'Yeah, not so bad, how about yourself?' 'Oh right, so off to America soon, that's brilliant. What about the job?' 'So still in the place in Croydon?' This sort of chatter could go on for hours and could leave her more lonely than if she'd been by herself in her flat, or in a bare prison cell in a desert. She didn't hate parties per se, she hated the denuded vision of sociability to which they usually catered. Or perhaps she was just doing it all very wrong. She wanted to be alone, not because she hated people, but because she craved a level of connection she didn't know how to secure.

Anna operated under the mistaken assumption that telling people her problems would necessarily repel and disgust them. Who would ever want to hear what she really felt? She did not, therefore, disclose much of her inner life and instead set herself up as a devoted and careful enquirer into the lives of others. Several people playfully called her their shrink. They complimented her on her pertinent questions. It wasn't untypical for those she was with to find that they had done most of the talking throughout an evening. She wasn't being coy or deceptive. She couldn't imagine that anyone would fail to be repulsed by a tour around her distinctive regions of pain.

Nevertheless, Anna wasn't solemn. She liked to be teased (in a gentle way) for everything that was ridiculous and overblown about her fears and hang-ups. She had a particular soft spot for a friend at school who had nicknamed her Miss Melancholy, and in honour of a brooding singer she had loved, Morrissey's girlfriend. She knew that her personality was exaggerated in unfortunate directions, she just didn't know how to correct her habits on her own. She longed for a day when, through another's kindly and buoyant interpretation, she might more regularly find herself as gently comedic as she felt she was, deep down.

Anna was a particular enthusiast of self-help books. She knew that this wasn't something to shout about, particularly among her more highbrow friends. Knowing how to live was supposed to be easy; who but an idiot could need a book that promised to be able to tell you how to feel more attractive, be confident, make sense of love and navigate your career? Yet Anna didn't mind owning up to her ignorance; none of that was remotely obvious to her. There were around 150 titles scattered around her apartment, many of them with passages heavily underlined. Other people might have the luxury of reading for pleasure, she was doing it for clues to her survival.

Anna made it back from the party after 1 a.m., just in time to encounter her other great hurdle in life. Insomnia meant her body was exhausted, but her mind still felt like holding on for a while in order to make sense of certain things that – vaguely but powerfully – needed unpicking; conversations she had had that evening, but more broadly, strands of her life that she found it hard to observe during daylight hours: her parents, her real goals, Jake, Joachim … Insomnia was her mind's revenge for all the thoughts she had been careful not to have in the day.

In the end, past 3 a.m., Anna had a very pleasant dream; she'd had this one before. It was her and her young child. They were in the park, playing. Her little girl might have been two or three. Anna felt suffused with tenderness for this small person she seemed to know very well. When she was awake, Anna refused the whole idea of children. They definitely weren't for her; she had insisted on this since she was a teenager. It wasn't that Anna didn't like children, she liked them far too much to imagine that someone like her could adequately cater for their needs. She had taken early retirement out of a heightened awareness of what all that poor parenting might do to a fragile and dependent human.

The Visit
Home

It was Saturday and Anna was on the 11.03 a.m. train to Colchester. She loved travelling when things were this empty; only her and two others in the whole carriage. A brand new train as well, with attractive grey upholstered seats, an even temperature and doors that closed with a quiet hiss. Her mind took on some of the expansiveness of the views outside. Barren fields and bleak estates, separated by stations whose names had lodged in her memory on her journeys down as a teenager: Stratford, Romford, Shenfield, Ingatestone. The train helped her to think; the journey in the outer world paving the way for one in the inner realm.

The birthday had, in the end, not been as bad as she had feared. That was the benefit of being a pessimist. Few things could ever really blindside you; most of the possible pain had been factored in way ahead of time. Anna had learnt to disappoint herself long before anyone else could have a go. Jake forgot a present but the dinner – a takeaway, as it turned out – had been nice enough. Several of her friends had called. She had made a few resolutions in her diary. Someone at work had bought her a book – *Unleash the Power Within* – which seemed packed with interesting ideas.

Her parents had said they would be waiting for her at the station. It was tiring to be going through this ambivalent rigmarole all over again. What a curse for Homo sapiens to have been lumbered with such an exceptionally long and susceptible period of maturation. The dates had been part of Anna's course: a foal can stand up thirty minutes after its birth, a golden eaglet grows up in twelve weeks, a chimpanzee is an adult in nine years. But at close to thirty, Anna was still dependent on the approval and kindness of the two ageing figures who had once conspired to put her on the earth.

The problem with how humans mature isn't just time, thought Anna, it's the vulnerability involved. It wouldn't matter if a baby turtle's mother was emotionally detached or if a golden eagle's dad had a propensity to humiliate or shout. But our species has no option but to take parental failings so much more to heart. An unfortunate set of events between the ages of zero and ten has the power to unbalance an entire life; a competitive parent can permanently sap a child's energy to succeed, a guilt-inducing one can breed a near-ineradicable sense of shame.

The train had picked up some delays. It looked as if she might be fifteen minutes late coming in. She hadn't managed to warn her parents and already the familiar anxiety had taken up. Her father was manic on the topic of punctuality. She remembered her fear from childhood. Every delay would be interpreted as a personally targeted insult, as if the postman, the airline or the garage were engaged in a well-concealed conspiracy to wound him. Shouting and slammed doors followed. Yet what had begun as his problem had – in the manner of these things – eventually become hers. She expected everyone to be as tempestuous and excitable as her early carer had been.

They were waiting for her on the platform: two huddled figures, surprisingly small, muttering something to one another, probably about the parking ticket or the change. She imagined for a second having a different history, walking past them and asking a taxi to take her to the other side of Colchester to an alternative set of parents, a responsible, benign retired High Court judge and a clever, patient secondary school teacher, who could have welcomed her progress in the world and been warm, reliable and helpful. As a child, she had never been far from the fantasy that she had been adopted.

The familiar road home. She anticipated every tree, road sign and house. She didn't even know she knew it but it was all stored somewhere inside the unconscious, requiring only a nudge to re-emerge. How much our minds contain without letting on; they forget very little in the end. The patter inside the car was as familiar: 'Yes, Mum, I did remember to send Auntie June a card.' 'No, Dad, it's just a new anorak and it's comfortable, so it's not a problem, but thank you for asking.' The usual combination of misplaced concern, aggression, invasiveness and neurosis, and on her side, the usual blend of irritation, guilt and sadness.

By the time they pulled up, her father was back to the subject of punctuality. Had she really not realised that she would be late? Isn't that the sort of thing that she could keep an eye on? Was it fair to worry her mother like this? What about the lunch? It would have to be significantly delayed … Somewhere inside him, there was the thing he was really worried about: some deep early wound of which these later ostensible subjects of worry were merely the flickering shadows. But there seemed no way to reach these without generating fruitless degrees of annoyance; he would go to the grave a stranger to most of what really ailed him.

They gave her a few moments to unpack her overnight things. She sat on her bed in her old room, untouched except for some towels that had been stored in her cupboard. She had spent hours here, lifetimes, the cluttered space the scene of so many intense emotions: fury, grief, lust, fear. She had lain on the bed and taken a call from a boy for the first time. She had sat at the desk and laboured for what felt like decades for her GCSEs and A levels. Tightly packed on a shelf were her worn set texts: Sylvia Plath, J.D. Salinger, Zadie Smith … What had all the strife and worry been for in the end?

She wanted to go back and comfort the teenager she had been. How serious that girl was, how inwardly panicked, how confused and alone. It was a great deal easier to feel sympathy for who she had been fifteen years ago than for who she was now. She would like to have taken the girl in her arms and reassured her that she was not dreaming, that things were unjustifiably strange and cruel, that she deserved more than this, that she would one day be free and have distance, that it would get better, in a way.

She thought too how beautiful that young girl had been – without in any way recognising it. So delicate and clever-looking, with lively curious eyes, exactly the sort of girl that she would be touched by if she saw her walking to school with a heavy rucksack in the darkness. Tears welled at the thought of all the lonely boys and girls up and down the country who were right at that moment sure only of how unacceptable and awful they were, with no one to comfort them or give them perspective. If only there was some way to help them. Her parents were right: she was a dreamer, and a strange and strangely emotional one at that.

'I'm coming,' Anna called out from the bedroom, wiping her tears. 'And why did no one remember to post these *again*?' she heard her father mutter to himself in the hallway. She felt the old impulse to appease him in his moods. 'I've come from London just in order to post them for you,' she called out. She knew how to use humour around angry people, especially men; she could charm and appease enraged lions. But there was nothing joyful about this skill – it had been a response to some deeply unreasonable situations. Perhaps many comics grow their talent at origin in order to get along with one or two implausibly serious people in the vicinity. It might be better though, thought Anna, if children could have the luxury to remain as stony-faced as they needed to.

This was the problem with children, she continued in her mind. There was no one they could appeal to for another take on what was supposed to be 'normal'. They couldn't doubt the situation they were in. The family of origin determined everything about their sense of good and bad, right and wrong, for a decade or more. How could a six-year-old ever develop the mental freedom to question what Mum or Dad did or declared? What was an eight-year-old to do in the face of a parent's strident insistence on this or that point of behaviour? The fault had to lie with oneself; *they* could never be the problem.

Anna was haunted by the power that grown-ups had over children. She couldn't bear to go near stories of child abuse in the media. That there were children being submitted to cruelty anywhere on earth made her feel sick and desperate; she had to shift her mind to something else quickly or she felt a panic descend. But worse, she knew that those headline cases were only the tip of a vast iceberg of pain, ranging from the obviously ghastly to the merely quietly, but still intensely dreadful. No, Anna was sure: she would never have children of her own. Ever.

It was a short car ride to the pub. Silences interspersed by an array of suspicious questions. The fields were bare and cold. It could be lovely here in the summer. 'No, Mum, I'm not senior enough in the company for that …' As a teenager she had loved to ride her bicycle from village to village, and occasionally find a field in which to lie down and watch the clouds pass overhead. 'Dad, they're not taking advantage of me, it's just the way it works in companies …' She thought how much she would love to leave London and live in a small cottage somewhere rural with someone she loved and felt peaceful around. She wouldn't allow herself to be sad forever.

It was one of her father's favourite remarks to her in restaurants: 'You can have anything you like on the menu.' Pause. 'The children's menu …' The unfunny joke pointed to a more serious theme. He never let her forget that he had provided for her, that he had once controlled money, that she had been entirely dependent on him materially, that he had worked hard all his life, and implicitly that there was a lot to be grateful for. It was in a sense true that she had never wanted for anything. They'd taken holidays abroad: Spain three times, Egypt once. Not bad for the daughter of a plumber who had – and the point was repeatedly made – left school at sixteen without a penny to his name. Sometimes it seemed wholly unclear to her whether she really had anything to complain about.

Anna decided to have the fish, Dad would have the sausages, Mum the chicken. What is a privileged childhood? Society likes to answer that one swiftly for us: foreign trips, a spacious bedroom, a comfortable home, plenty of presents. But true privilege might be something else entirely: careful listening, affectionate nicknames, patience, a tolerance for stumbles, an interest in minor sorrows and pains, a generosity of interpretation around difficult behaviour, a sense of existing in one's full complexity in another's mind. And as Anna had a hard time focusing on, one kind of privilege might cleverly be wielded to mask the absence of another.

In her mid-teens, two of Anna's good friends had rebelled spectacularly against their parents: one – the daughter of the headmaster – had shaved her head, got a tattoo and joined the Communist Party. The other had taken to smoking weed and had several times told her parents to fuck off to their faces. It frightened and delighted Anna in equal measure. These rebellions might have looked defiant but they were underpinned by a secure knowledge that, deep down, the parents cared profoundly – and would ultimately take whatever was thrown at them. How loved and cherished one would have to feel in order to be able to scream mercilessly at one's parents that one had never asked to be born. That was true unalloyed privilege!

Anna had never felt remotely secure enough to risk telling her parents that she hated them – or was, at least, extremely frustrated and hurt by their moments of narrow-mindedness and insensitivity. It wasn't outright anger that she dreaded being met with, rather a haughty and more devastating indifference. When she was little, her parents had openly stated that they had far better things to worry about than a troublesome child. 'Go and find other parents if you're going to be like this,' her mother would tell her whenever she became, as she put it, 'difficult'. It was a strategy of genius: love your children devotedly and they'll act up; ignore and undermine them, they'll be meekly and politely obsessed with you for life.

Expressed another way, Anna had failed to have an adolescence. Teenage years can be marked by so much self-dramatisation, absurdity and pretention that it's easy to miss their value. What really goes on beneath their escapades and rigmaroles is a search for how to be real. The rebellious adolescent is taking a chance – through their acts of defiance – to discover their authentic self and to push back against arbitrary and nonsensical demands. The value of being able to do so stretches beyond the moment itself; it guarantees a lifelong ability to assert one's needs and articulate genuine desires and interests. 'Yes, Mum, the fish is really lovely, thank you. How is your chicken?'

Anna's mother took a great interest in small children who were, as she liked to put it, 'good'. 'Look at that family over there, the children haven't complained once,' she noted, gesturing towards two angelic-seeming children, colouring in a book while their parents finished their meal. By association, she then remembered the grandchild of a colleague, no more than a month old, whom she had recently met and described as 'a little chap, good as gold, who knows who the boss is'. This was too much even for Anna. 'Mum, I hope this young man discovers his voice very soon and rages and howls as much as he needs to.' Anna's mother didn't rise to the occasion; she fell silent, looked into the middle distance, and waited for this moment of uncharacteristic insurrection to subside.

The great rarely mentioned detail – and origin of much of the agony – was that Anna had not been the first. Two years before her birth, there had been a little boy, who had been longed for, anticipated and adored from the initial ultrasound. The boy had not, however, made it. The stillborn child – Anna didn't know his name – had been given a proper funeral and lay somewhere in a churchyard not far from the house. Anna both knew this and didn't really, in the manner of all great family secrets. The legacy of her brother was a permanent impression that couldn't ever be discussed or expurgated; that her birth had been premised on someone else's death; that the mere fact of her existence posed, at some level, an existential problem and offence.

What got Anna through were animals. She had loved them as long as she could remember: small ones like earthworms and beetles, larger ones like a neighbour's Jack Russell and far bigger ones like the horses in the stables at the end of the lane where she'd gone riding every weekend for a decade. She even thought rather a lot about exotic creatures like llamas and okapis. She understood technically, as an adult, that none of them could ever actually love her back, but that had never seemed too important (or in the end plausible). Her face lit up in their presence. She felt moved by pretty much any creature she might come across. She was always close to an 'awww' and an abstract desire to give an animal a hug. Children can be geniuses at working out what they need to make it through.

In the car on the way home the conversation turned to Jake. Though neither parent had much liked him on the only occasion they had met him, his name had started to come up often – as a way, Anna felt, to cast doubt on her abilities and judgement and to probe indirectly at her longer-term plans.

'Is he intending to work in an office one day?'

'Have you met his parents?'

'Does he go on these trips of his on his own?'

'Does he pay taxes?'

But what in the end decisively ignited the argument that had been in the air for at least the previous hour was an enquiry from Anna's mother that she delivered just as they were pulling into the drive: 'Does he actually know how old you are?'

She had more or less held it together in the face of several provocations, but this was too much. Her anger didn't go beyond: 'Of course he does', followed by a walk to her room (for 'a rest') and a firmly shut door. But there could naturally have been a whole slew of swear words that she might have added and a good slam, too – had there not been a dead brother, years of submission, an ingrained sense of worthlessness and ample doses of masochism. Rage was not Anna's style. She lay on her childhood duvet (a picture of an Andalusian mare on the front) and cried once more. Not much had changed at home, really.

Soon after, Anna went into the kitchen and announced that she'd have to go back to London unexpectedly. A friend of hers had forgotten her key and needed her help. It was an obviously nonsensical excuse but it suited everyone to pretend to believe in it. As Anna was packing her bag, her mother had obviously allowed herself the observation that Anna shouldn't be quite so sensitive and should try to be more forgiving towards other human beings who might mean well towards her. By this stage, Anna had returned to her long-standing position of not hoping to be understood to any significant degree under this roof of origin. 'You're right, Mum, thanks. I'll try my best. I'll text you when I arrive.'

She and her father were almost silent on the way to the station. She was grateful for every change of gear and sound of the indicator. It was the weight of all that was never said that crushed her every time. Why was there so much hostility? What had she done to these people? Why could she never get it right? She felt her eyes fill again.

'I think I'll be able to catch it, Dad. It doesn't matter if it's not the fast one. I've got a book with me.' They were almost there now. 'We'll keep in touch. Stay well, Dad. Thanks for the lift.'

And still, despite all this, she loved both of them more than she could admit.

There was, in the end, some time before the train left. From inside the carriage, she looked out and saw her father, who had walked onto the bridge across from where her train stood to give her a shy wave. He could be very sweet, in his own way, and that was some of the problem. Out and out monsters would have been easier to overcome. It was this devil-ish mixture of meanness and attention, stupidity and kindness, that was so difficult to make sense of. If they had just been dreadful she would have been able to get them out of her mind a long while ago.

As the train pulled out, she gave her own small, shy wave back. Across the aisle from her in the carriage there was a couple close to her parents' age. They had the same sort of clothes and were talking in recognisable ways. He wanted an apple, she was getting it out of her bag; there was a fuss about a paper napkin. Flaws of character, which if one came across in other people would be entirely undisturbing, could – thought Anna – prove wholly disastrous when they manifested themselves under the intensely demanding conditions of parenthood. Such is the responsibility of the job, under its pitiless glare, a minor flaw could have a catastrophic impact – like a pebble in a pair of marathon shoes or a coin in a jet engine. A bit of selfishness, a slight rigidity, a touch of fussiness or ill-temper, things so easy to overlook in an ordinary person, could in a parent serve to wound a child for life.

Her mother was in a sense right – she was too sensitive. But to be someone's child is inevitably to be more sensitive to them than one will be towards almost anyone else one will ever encounter across the years; no one else will again have such a power to harm or help us. A preternatural openness is baked into the basic terms of the relationship. A question like: 'Does he actually know how old you are?' might pursue her for decades. (It joined other comments like: 'You're not as interesting to other people as you seem to believe' and 'No one likes a cry baby'.) She could have forgiven her parents so much – if only they had not been her parents.

What particularly puzzled Anna were her parents' attitudes to success and failure. On the one hand, she was under pressure to do well: she needed to get good marks at school, to do a noteworthy job, to have a respectable family life. And yet, actual success seemed also to be a problem. As she noted, her parents didn't actually want to hear that her colleagues thought well of her, they appeared threatened by mentions of anything glamorous in her London life, there were repeated hints that she might be getting ahead of herself. It was as though in the end neither success nor failure would do. There wasn't really any chair for her to sit on. She couldn't be a loser or a winner in her parents' befuddling imaginations.

Before leaving her old bedroom, she had noticed a picture of herself on the pinboard above her desk and slipped it into her bag. She took it out and studied it closely, breaking off every now and then to look out the window at the darkening landscape. They'd be reaching London's suburbs soon. She would have been five or six, the fussy child of her mother's description, but also a little one full of questions and joys and unexpected courage. How long it might take to understand her; she was only at the very start of making sense of who this impish girl had really been – and of knowing how to help her with her complicated emotional inheritance.

The Crisis

Anna called Jake as soon as she reached home.

'Hi babe, I wasn't expecting you back till tomorrow. All OK with the parents? Did they ask sweetly after their beloved future son-in-law? God your mother's sexy when she wants to be. Did she have her usual black boots on again?'

He made her smile even when she really didn't want to. She was tired and craved a bath. She had been travelling for close to five hours since morning. Except that this time, she had a particular sense of unease around Jake. Something in his manner was off: hurried, distracted, embarrassed, evasive.

It suddenly dawned on her: 'Are you alone?'

The usual prevarications and obfuscations followed.

'Alone? In what way? I mean, yes, of course. Why not? Definitely. Alone for now.'

It was the same old bullshit and she knew it. She had always known it. Why did he 'travel' so much? Why was his phone so often disabled? Who were those women who liked his posts? She had been in flight from the truth from the start. She simply hadn't respected herself enough to dare to demand that she be enough for him.

'Do you want me to come over, babe?'

Silence from her end.

'Are you sure? You sound upset; are things really OK?'

She didn't answer for a long while. She was newly uninterested in papering over the cracks; why not let the discomfort hang for as long as it needed to? Why was she always the one to fill in the blanks for other people, to make excuses for them and to save them from their own embarrassment and cruelty?

She had had enough. 'Jake, go to hell and don't try to call me.' She hung up and blocked his number.

Anna didn't sleep well that night. She was up between two and four. That was the problem with self-assertion, there was always a kickback from an inner voice that didn't like defiance very much and had other messages to promote: *Know your place. Who are you to cause a fuss? No one likes a shrew.* She got into work early. There was a presentation to a client at midday and she wanted a chance to go over the slides and practice her words. But when she arrived, there was a note on her desk from her boss: *Anna, could you drop in to see me at ten? There's something we should discuss – in private.*

The inkblot test by the Swiss psychologist Hermann Rorschach: the blotches don't mean any one thing; the ambiguity draws out one's projections, one sees one's own characteristic fears, desires and fantasies in them. The timid person will see monsters; the sexual one will spot vaginas; the paranoid one will identify only enemies. The boss's note was a Rorschach test all of its own. One could see in it principally whatever happened to be inside oneself, which meant that for Anna, this wasn't a request for a meeting. It was a discrete declaration of an intention to sack her.

A Voice of One's Own

'Anna, you're doing so well. I couldn't be any happier. I just hope you're enjoying your time with us.'

Anna felt light-headed and wondered if she might faint. The lack of sleep was catching up with her. Her stomach wasn't particularly calm either.

'But there is one thing I wanted to mention.'

Now it was coming, of course.

'I think that sometimes with clients, you could afford to make your points with just a bit more enthusiasm. People like eye contact a lot in this business. And smiling always works too. I think you understand exactly what I mean. It's a small thing but it would be great if you can take it on board going forward.'

She went to the park to settle herself. There was what he had said, and then there was what he had meant, which was something else entirely. The real meaning ran in a very different direction, Anna knew it: 'Often I think about what a piece of shit you are: so grim faced, so pathetic with clients. I've thought about telling you this on many occasions. I've giggled about you with my partner. Sometimes, I look at you and feel pity. The desperation, the neediness, the ridiculous shaped head, the acne. I need you to help make money but my God I feel sorry for you.' With a certain kind of childhood behind one, no wonder one might feel a little defensive.

Anna couldn't find her equilibrium in the coming days. The presentation went well, very well some people said, but it wasn't enough to calm her. Jake had found an old email address for her and sent her a dozen messages – before she found a way to block him there too. Her sleep was fitful. She was up at least three hours every night and felt every missing hour throughout the following day. Seeing her at her desk one lunchtime, a kindly colleague asked if she was feeling OK. That ended up being the required prompt. She had accrued a lot of extra holidays since she had started – and the office was set to be quiet until the end of the month. Catching him in the hallway, she asked her boss if she might take the following week off.

She had no wish to go anywhere. She ordered in some groceries and stayed in bed. Sometimes she slept, usually at odd hours, at other points, she lay very still in a kind of daydream. She saw messages arriving on her phone and ignored them all. Her mind seemed to be circling certain large ideas without ever being able to settle on them. But she needed the quiet. She felt numb. There was a metallic taste in her mouth and a throbbing near her temples. One night in the early hours, she discovered an online diagnostic tool, which promised to make sense of her symptoms. There were thirty rather detailed questions on this and that. And then came the verdict: Anna was apparently – to listen to this particular source – in the process of having a nervous breakdown.

The term felt terrifying but the website was quick to throw a different light on the matter. A breakdown was not – so the argument ran – any kind of long-term harbinger of doom. It could, if things were handled correctly, be a helpful and necessary step towards a genuine and tolerable recovery. She wasn't spiralling into insanity, she just had certain new discoveries to make about herself. She had been wandering the world oblivious to all manner of tensions and incoherencies that the breakdown might help to resolve. Anna sat up in bed and copied down a section of the website in her journal.

Beneath the breakdown, a long-repressed truth may be trying to break through layers of deception. When a person is unable to function 'normally', it may be because 'normality' has grown riddled with something mean and impossible. The breakdown is a bid for health masquerading as an illness. The illness acts as our conscience; it won't let up until we have figured out the truth. It can't tell us the truth by itself, but it is urging us to make the effort to find it out. The insomnia, paranoia or despair are there to keep us honest. The illness's contract with us is: understand me, and I will leave you alone; ignore me, and I will upset normality to prevent you from deceiving yourself any longer. Illness can be the midwife of truth.

The fortunate ones among us manage to decode the riddle. We have fallen ill because we have been victims of tensions and paradoxes, which we have needed the cover of 'madness' to be able to look at. We aren't really ill at all – we may be closer to sanity than we have ever dared to imagine. And then there was a small piece of advice at the end: *You may want to seek the services of a psychotherapist to discuss these issues further.*

She had – privately – been suspicious of psychotherapy from the outset. She understood its ostensible benefits, some of her friends spoke highly of it, many of the books she read recommended it. But its protocols ran directly counter to a few deeply established facets of her character. Anna was not someone who wanted to sit and tell a stranger her sorrows; she was far too guarded and ashamed for that. Who could bear to listen to her stories anyway? What she had to say was unremittingly boring, drab and silly. She was making most of it up anyway. She was fine.

Once, at university, shortly before she'd left, she had succumbed and gone to see someone. Not a psychotherapist, but a counsellor trained in the techniques of cognitive behavioural therapy, which drew her in because it proclaimed that it might be entirely unnecessary to look into the past in order to understand the difficulties of the present.

'I won't be asking you about your childhood or anything like that,' the counsellor had helpfully proclaimed with a nervous smile at the outset – and turned out to be true to his word. That felt very right indeed to Anna.

Unfortunately, the counselling sessions had not been especially helpful. They had given her a host of practical tips to deal with her anxieties. Shortly before a party or a meeting that worried her, she had been advised to repeat three things to herself – and perhaps write them down somewhere on her phone. The first point had something to do with defining the fear, which was compared to a lion or a tiger. Then she had to lasso the fear so as to get the lion or tiger to stop pacing. Then, she had to count to eight, or perhaps ten, but the details grew hazy and Anna had not, in fact, ever properly put the technique into practice.

You may want to seek the services of a psychotherapist to discuss these issues further. The sentence didn't leave her alone the next day. Nor the one after that. Sometimes it incensed her. Why should she have to seek such services? The advice seemed bossy, intrusive but also niggling and impossible to ignore. Who were these therapist people? What did they know about her? How would she find one anyway? But pain has a habit of getting us to do what we would neglect in more comfortable circumstances. She eventually plucked a name almost at random from the internet and made an appointment for 5 p.m. the following Tuesday – an office an eight-minute walk from her home. It was ridiculous really, especially because, in the end, there wasn't even anything wrong with her.

The Shrink

Dr Devi had her office at the back of a Chinese restaurant on the high street. Despite the central location it was extremely quiet. There was a large magnolia tree in the courtyard and the sound of birds in the garden next door. Inside on the walls, there were pictures of Hindu deities whose names Anna didn't know, a set of the works of Donald Winnicott and a large couch, which Anna chose not to sit on, preferring one of two arm-chairs instead.

Anna announced from the outset that she would not be here long; a couple of sessions probably, three at the outer limit. She wasn't someone who wanted to 'drone on about her problems' or 'take up someone's valuable time with my nonsense'. Dr Devi's face remained impassive, though one could have detected a hint of a warm, understanding smile.

After Anna had outlined a few more reasons why she wouldn't be coming to therapy very much, Dr Devi remarked: 'Why don't we see how you feel, and let that be our guide?'

It was such a common sense, modest observation that Anna immediately breathed a sigh of relief. Why wouldn't she, in fact, allow herself to see how she felt? She hadn't done that in a long while. Her impulse was to try to work out any situation way ahead of time in order to tame it of every uncertainty. Spontaneity was not – evidently – her game.

'Remember, this is about you and what you might need,' added Dr Devi with what was now an unambiguous smile.

This felt so kind and so humane that despite herself, and much to her irritation, Anna felt a familiar tension in her nose that presaged the onset of tears.

Dr Devi looked on with an infinitely generous expression as Anna wept. She wasn't going to make her feel remotely bad for her previous declarations. She passed over a box of tissues. She understood. She seemed to understand a lot. She appeared to see very deep into Anna.

'Maybe you've been through many things,' said Dr Devi. 'And I think that you and I can allow ourselves to take a little look, at our own pace.'

More sobbing, after which Anna looked up sheepishly and said: 'I think I could come back here quite often; that might be nice for me …'

Knowing that she had another appointment was a comfort, but in the days that followed, Anna's mood plunged further than it had ever done. She felt overwhelmed, even choked, by a sense of how awful she was. It was as though a furious, cruel side of her was passing its verdict on her and would not let up with its condemnations: she was a disgrace, revolting, repulsive, disgusting … The adjectives lacked imagination but they were insistent and relentless. Sometimes, in response to their hammer blows, it seemed that killing herself would be the only way out.

The actual mechanisms of self-extinction were beyond her. Anna would never leap off a cliff or throw herself under a train. The pain and the mess made her shudder. She knew she would not have the strength required. At the same time, when her thoughts were giving her a lot of trouble, she longed never to have been born. She wanted to be in an endless sleep. If she had been given a button that could miraculously have removed her from the planet without causing difficulty to anyone, she would have pressed it without hesitation.

She was permanently afraid in a way that made no particular sense. She was reluctant to go out into the streets in case people saw her and she angered them. She felt ashamed to buy milk in the corner shop; why was she so lazy and greedy? Didn't she have something better to do? She imagined that anyone who came across her would hate her, that they might be saying awful things about her, pointing to her and referring to her as a waster, a liar and a weirdo. At work they were probably laughing – perhaps on social media – people had started to gossip. Strangers and acquaintances alike were united in finding her the most contemptible human being who had ever lived.

What relief she found came from running herself very long, hot baths. She took as many as three a day and lay in the water for over an hour every time. She felt safe in her steamy cocoon. No one could come in, there was nothing she had to do. She could just float calmly while trying to hold her mind steady to topics that didn't involve fear or self-hatred. She hadn't imagined that baths could be so essential to her fragile mind; she wondered how people like her had managed before they'd been around.

Anna knew only too well that her condition would strike most people as ridiculous. Whatever lip service polite society might pay to the idea of 'mental illness', her states of mind were, to anyone who hadn't been through something similar themselves, wholly beyond comprehension or sympathy. What on earth was really wrong? Why couldn't she pull herself together? She lacked for nothing materially, her country was at peace, she had a nice enough job … Why complain? But such logic was in the end like running one's hand over the stomach of an outwardly healthy young person and sceptically asking whether there could really be something called pancreatic cancer growing inside.

Dr Devi was interested in the violence with which Anna spoke to herself.

'Tell me,' she asked very lightly (she moved with the utmost delicacy; a ballerina in a china shop), 'what do you think people might say if they saw you here in therapy?'

'Here?' Anna said and laughed. 'That's not hard: that I'm very weird, that I'm mad, that I'm self-indulgent, that I'm trying to cover up for my failures, that I'm begging for sympathy, that I'm attempting to win you over to my side so that you can feel sorry for me.'

There was another pause (there were lots of pauses with Dr Devi): 'You're very hard on yourself, Anna, aren't you? Very hard indeed.'

The idea had never especially struck her; Anna dwelt too much inside the dynamic of her harshness to notice the extent to which she was its victim. But now Dr Devi mentioned it, it was easier to see. Yes, thought Anna, she was probably pretty hard on herself. But no sooner had this idea taken hold than a follow-up thought entered her mind: that she definitely deserved to be this hard. After all, she complained so much, she made such a fuss, she was so stupid and so arrogant. Yes, concluded Anna, she *was* hard on herself. But for a range of very good reasons.

The next session, Anna recounted an incident at school – she would have been sixteen – in which her girlfriends had turned on her and begun a campaign of mockery against her for sleeping with a boy sooner than she might.

'I was the school slag for a while,' replied Anna without any emotion. 'They kept throwing my books out of the window.' The way in which Anna recounted stories of her life to Dr Devi often had a dispassionate coldness to it that seemed to astonish the therapist and made her want to compensate for it.

'How horrible that must have been,' said Dr Devi. 'That must have been so upsetting.'

But Anna was nonplussed. 'No, not really. These things happen at rough schools. I probably deserved it. I really was a bit of a slag then …'

Dr Devi attempted a different tack. 'Tell me, Anna, if you were not you, if there was a vulnerable sixteen-year-old girl and she happened to exercise less than complete caution around a boy, what do you think should happen to her? Do you think her books should be thrown out of the window by her erstwhile friends, who would then also refer to her as a slag?'

The answer seemed obvious, put that way. 'Of course not,' replied Anna, 'Poor thing, I'd really want to protect her and make sure she was OK.'

'Well, then, why isn't such treatment normal and fair when it comes to you?'

Anna's mind went blank. 'I'm not sure, I'm really not sure …'

They were still at the start of the journey; they might have had ten sessions already. This was not work for the impatient. It was a sign of the scale of Anna's distress that she continued to feel like coming, despite the time, cost and sheer strangeness of it all. One session, they started to talk of the nausea, the one that kicked in whenever Anna threatened to do well at work. Together they started to identify a voice in her mind that grew insistent the more she succeeded. The voice was threatening and bullying; it had the gnarl of a rabid dog that wanted to tear into her: *Who do you think you are? We're going to get you for this. Don't you dare to be an arrogant brat. Know your place.*

From the outside, one might have said that Anna 'lacked confidence'. But that explanation missed the scale of the inner conflict of which a meek manner was simply the outward result. Anna was not without ambition or desire to triumph. In fact, she yearned to make more of herself. The problem was that another side of her mind seemed appalled by any degree of self-assertion and appeared determined to bring her down. The angry dog side wanted to rip into her the minute she acted impressively – and filled her mind with paranoia and self-recrimination. She ended up meek and cowed to escape something in her that wanted so badly to succeed.

Anna and Dr Devi together noticed another pattern. Whenever Anna did well at something (felt attractive, made a friend, did well at work), there was always – to an extent Anna hadn't previously reflected on – a price to be paid. Within forty-eight hours, something inside her would be thrown off balance. She would grow beset by worries, she would ruminate in self-hating ways. It was as if by winning in some area or another, she was in danger of defying a law according to which she was living, a prohibition against a worthwhile life. Something inside her didn't like victory one bit.

Somewhere around their fifteenth session, Dr Devi made a direct suggestion (she made these very seldom). There were, she thought, as it were, different 'voices' in Anna's head. Not actual voices but ways of speaking – and some of these did not belong to her, in a way. Some of these voices were – if she could put it in this strange manner – voices that she might have inherited from people around her, especially, perhaps, from her earliest caregivers. Furthermore, these voices were not particularly kind ones. When she called herself a piece of shit who shouldn't exist, this was not – Dr Devi proposed – Anna speaking to Anna. It was a version of someone she had known well long ago doing so.

It was a tribute to Dr Devi's skill that this admittedly outlandish idea did not meet with immediate rejection. Anna was self-aware enough to recognise that she did sometimes judge herself in ways that surprised her and could use voices that were harder and more pitiless than she might consider reasonable. The thought that she was awful and needed to die did, in a sense, seem to come from somewhere else. The point of difference Anna had with Dr Devi was in assessing whose voices these might originally have been.

Surprisingly, Anna's mother had been supremely sweet to her since the failed visit home. She'd sided with her plan to take some time off, and when Anna had eventually returned to work (part-time), she had checked in regularly on her progress. She'd even sent her a homemade cake, a banana loaf of the sort she'd loved as a child. So when the subject of inner voices came up, it was clear to Anna whose voices these might or might not be. She told Dr Devi at some length about a hard-to-please teacher at school. And about a windsurfing instructor on a Devon holiday. These were the origins of the voices.

When it came to her parents, Anna suddenly felt powerfully benevolent towards them. She told Dr Devi that her father had left school with few qualifications and yet had managed to build up a successful plumbing business. She talked about her mother's work as a receptionist in a GP surgery and the gratitude of her patients for her kind manner. She even mentioned the holiday that her parents had taken her on to Egypt when she was eleven, and how there was a buffet in the hotel from which she'd been allowed to take as much as she wanted. Some days, Dr Devi's job was far from simple.

This is what Dr Devi knew: when a child is small, it is very difficult for her to find her parents 'bad'. There may be a lot of bad things going on in the house: shouting, belittlement, neglect, aggression and much worse, but the child is in no position to understand the real motives at play. She is too dependent on her parents to think clearly, she has nowhere else to turn, she has to cope with the situation as it is. She is therefore faced with a choice. Someone is bad: either her or her parents. And at this juncture, the issue is almost always very simple. There is no real question about it.

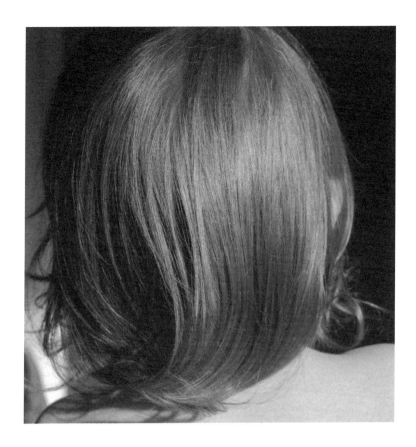

Dad is shouting – she must have done something wrong. He has broken the latch on the front door by slamming it very hard, but there was something she should have done to spare him his rage. Mum is sarcastic and bullying, but she, the child, must have annoyed her mother with something very silly she'd said. Both parents are ignoring her. However, she doesn't deserve attention. She's been called an ungrateful brat, but she has missed how kind her caregivers are. To every piece of difficult treatment, the child ascribes an explanation that places herself – and some putative failing or another – as the cause. This isn't egoism, it's a poignant, doomed attempt to make the best out of an unbearable situation. It's a bid for hope.

So long as the child has only herself to blame, then there is a possibility of change and therefore of an eventual end to suffering. She could try harder not to be so silly. She could redouble her efforts to be polite. She could attempt to do better at school. She could work harder on her marks. She might try to delight her parents by one day having a brilliant job. She could do something to calm the aggression that she has in some way unleashed through her badness. And then, at last, she could be happy. The desperate child exchanges the right to anger for a compulsion to self-criticism.

The mentality – though it grew somewhat more sophisticated with time – had remained with Anna all her life. As long as she could remember, she had wanted to do 'better'. She had tried impossibly hard at sport, then at school. She had spent hours at her desk in an attempt to get the sort of grades that would lead to a good report – and then, hopefully, contented parents. Her search for approval had eventually spread outwards. She now wanted to please bosses, boyfriends, colleagues – all in an attempt to wipe away a basic sense of badness that had infected her essence from the start.

Whenever we meet with someone who is convinced they are not enough, who believes fervently that there is something very wrong with them, who has no faith in their abilities, who doubts everything they say … we cannot any longer get away with describing them as 'unconfident'. We have to identify their behaviour as a legacy of an original situation in which someone else found them not enough, someone else gave them a sense that they were insufficient, someone else doubted what they had to say. Behind every 'underconfident' individual lies a family drama we haven't yet had the opportunity to understand properly.

To make the slightest criticism of her parents in front of Dr Devi was for Anna to challenge a mental structure that she had clung to since her earliest years. It didn't come easily. It was so much more tempting to hate oneself than to be annoyed with someone else. Her loyalty to her progenitors was immense and unyielding. Though she allowed herself the odd criticism at a surface level, in her heart of hearts, she was still her parents' unyielding devotee; she was as unquestioning as a religious adherent. They remained – in some primitive dimension – her gods and she needed to do better, a lot better, to calm down their justified ire and disappointment.

Quite why Anna's parents were as they were, Dr Devi pointed out, was impossible for the two of them to guess at with any great accuracy from the vantage point of the psychotherapy room. They could only speculate vaguely – but that might be enough. They could imagine that there must have been certain very big problems in both of their pasts, that was self-evident. Her father appeared to have a huge rage against the world for not treating him with dignity. His own father had crushed and neglected him, his older brother had sucked away most of the attention. Her mother had run away at sixteen from an abusive father and a weak mother; she had survived by becoming invulnerable and sarcastic, with no patience for her own, let alone others', sorrows. They had both not been very well and had found a fellow secret sufferer.

Child Anna had posed a grave emotional challenge to both parents through her unavoidable defencelessness and need. She had had no option but to cry out at night for milk and reassurance; she couldn't help but get all her early spellings wrong and to break crockery and clumsily knock into things in the bathroom. She was, by definition, incompetent, scared and in need of a lot of nurture, all of which would have posed some insuperable inner challenges to both parents. In the child they had created, they refound all the helplessness and incompetence they had so wanted to expunge from their lives. By targeting Anna, they had been able safely to locate the bad in someone else. They could be clever because she was stupid; they could feel strong because she was so weak.

Dr Devi was quick to add: none of this was obvious. Anna wasn't stupid for missing it. Families go to awe-inspiring lengths to hide what is going on inside them. The whitewash is thorough and pervasive, because the badness is largely unconscious even to its own perpetrators. Anna's parents were never going to be able to admit that they had needed to crush her to escape their own feelings of helplessness. The thought was as strange as it was in the end easy to evade; it could so easily be attacked as 'psychobabble'. Shrinks were ripe targets for mockery. No, they weren't a family in which anything like this went on. They had a paddling pool in the garden in the summer, they bought Anna a cat when she was seven, they went on a holiday to Egypt when she was eleven …

And yet, beneath the surface, there had been mixed messages that could scramble and break a mind. *Don't be weak, but we will be threatened by you if you achieve independence. Don't humiliate us with your failure, but we will be annoyed by your success. We adore you but we also despise your fragility. We want to look after you, but we resent any real needs you might show us.* It was in a sense rather reasonable that Anna should – over the years – have gone slightly out of her mind.

Still, it felt hideous for Anna to upturn any of the traditional narrative she had grown up with. She really didn't want to break her loyalty. There was no instant relief at all in the idea that in key areas her parents had not been able to want the best for her, had been too damaged not to want to wound her, had actively needed her to fail and to suffer. And yet, as Dr Devi pointed out, daring to look at her childhood in a new way offered the chance of a less oppressive life going forward: there might be an alternative to submission and self-laceration.

Anna's work with Dr Devi allowed her to think in a different way about bullies. She recognised that she had long been prey to being bullied; manhandled and treated unfairly by others. There had been characters at school, then certain boyfriends … She gave off signals that she couldn't defend herself. Her experiences at home had scrambled her ability to think clearly about what was her fault and what might be someone else's. She had been so busy defending her tormentors, she had lost sight of right and wrong, white and black. She couldn't now detect when someone was behaving badly towards her – let alone take her own side against them.

Anna began to understand aspects of her paranoia. Because there was hatred and fear that had had original, legitimate targets at home, and because these targets had been entirely off limits, they had been unmoored and made to circulate freely in her imagination, eventually attaching themselves to distant and innocent targets. She had to fear random things (the aggression of strangers in the street or in shops, the sudden malevolence of colleagues) because she hadn't been allowed to fear and mourn what, and who, had really been aggressive towards her at the start.

There was a sentence from the psychoanalyst Donald Winnicott to which Dr Devi drew Anna's attention: 'The catastrophe you fear *will* happen has *already* happened.' Anna feared that she would be disgraced, unmasked, brought down, mocked – and left humiliated and unloved. But she dreaded these things so powerfully because they had – in a sense – previously unfolded in a past about which she had not been able to reflect properly. Her present fears were a map as to the most traumatic incidents of a childhood that had been too arduous properly to study.

There were clues in the past too as to Anna's restlessness. She had always felt that what she had done was not 'enough'. She had never secured herself the right school grades. At the office, she had never won her company enough business. And in the broader scheme of her life, she could not relax and enjoy a holiday or period of respite. But this sense of not being enough was not written in stone; it had a history that could be unpicked. It was the result of never being able to please those who might have loved her. How could she feel she was enough if she had not been enough to those who had created her?

There was a bridge here to Anna's dead sibling. Anna rarely thought about him but Dr Devi surmised that Anna's mother must have fallen into an unprocessed depression following the loss of her child, leaving infant Anna confusedly feeling that her mother was elsewhere, distracted and unable to look after or delight in her adequately. This would have sparked intense feelings of being unacceptable and unwanted. Infant Anna had then attempted to awaken her depressed mother through a range of forlorn strategies, which she pursued in disguised forms to this day.

Partly, Anna had tried to 'awaken' her mother by being extremely good and outwardly impressive. Then she had tried to earn her mother's sympathy by failing in her career and falling into despair and crisis, but neither of these moves had had anything like the desired effects. Whether Anna won or lost, it seemed that her mother remained unable to notice or nurture her as would have been fitting; a part of her mind was somehow stuck in that little graveyard where her firstborn was buried. Dr Devi lamented the tragedy of it, but she also suggested to Anna that it would be another tragedy altogether if she was now unable to recognise, and move on, from it.

One didn't have to search too far either for clues as to Anna's feelings about her appearance. The real danger was not that she was ugly, as she so often feared; the actual terror was that she might be beautiful and extremely enticing to people and could, thereby, threaten a mother who could not abide to be challenged and usurped. Finding herself unattractive and dressing down were defences against a fateful envy and rivalry. She had needed to find herself ugly to ensure her mother's continued good mood; she had taken early retirement from her beauty to avoid upsetting a competitive rival in her own family.

From many of the sessions with Dr Devi, Anna emerged into the high street as if in possession of a highly dangerous set of secrets. She felt she had unearthed things that no one had ever wanted her to know, or guessed that she would be able to reach. She was untangling coils of wire that had been intricately knotted many years before. It was difficult work, but also liberating and energising in the extreme. Anna sometimes childishly wondered if it was even legal to be doing this. At certain moments, she felt better than she had ever done before.

Recovery

Things were changing in Anna's life. Not always very fast and there were plenty of reversals, but the mood was – on a good day – notably less desperate. She could still sometimes be nauseous at work when the pressure increased and expectations mounted, but she was better able to ignore her feelings of panic and foreboding. She knew that the alarms that sounded in her mind did not have to be taken as accurate. They had never been properly wired nor calibrated; they couldn't detect genuine dangers, a gust of wind might set them off, and so she might afford to ignore certain of their insistent wailings. There was perhaps a lot less to be frightened of than her gut would ever let her know.

Anna had come to appreciate how many of her counterproductive patterns of behaviour had their origins in a period of life without any remaining connection to the present; she was too often still fighting the battles of twenty years ago. There was no longer any need to sabotage her career in order to try to appease parental envy or stir her mother from her emotional lethargy. She could stop worrying about how she looked now that she knew that her physical underconfidence was the residue of maternal envy or disgust. She could repatriate her grief and feel more of what was necessary and true in the here and now.

A by-product of heightened insight was a wish to look after herself with greater kindness. She was in the habit of currying favour with precisely the kind of people who didn't believe in her and had to them a distant or hostile air; her interest was never more peaked than by doubters. It now struck her as absurd to wonder pitifully why her enemies didn't approve of her; she could stop abasing herself at the feet of cold, envious or neglectful types. They knew nothing of her and held none of her secrets. She could at last start to act rationally in relation to those who hated her: hate them back fast. And forget about them even faster.

She became bolder about upsetting people. In the past, she had tried hard to avoid inconveniencing anyone – especially those who pained her through their selfishness and inattention. But there were, she realised, no prizes in the next life for this form of self-sacrifice. If a joke wasn't funny, perhaps she didn't need to laugh. If someone was trampling across her interests, she might dare to complain. She could say she was busy and turn down an invitation. She could say she was too busy to take on a piece of work and lay down her boundaries with colleagues. She could displease – and survive.

Anna had told Dr Devi so many ostensibly embarrassing and private things about herself; she grew less inhibited about sharing more of her problems with others. She didn't only have to tell people about what was going well in her life, she could reveal her terrors and failures, too. She might not have to try so hard to seem 'normal' to earn affection. People might like to see more of her 'madness' – and to share theirs in turn. Confession was an act of generosity. Friendship didn't have to involve swapping news of how nice everything was. It could turn into a comforting arena in which to sigh and despair together at the sadness and horror of it all.

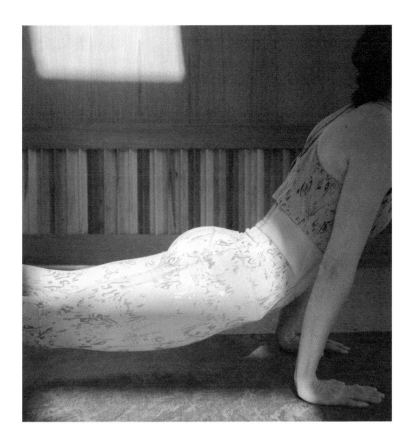

The question of her appearance ceased to have such a mesmerising hold on Anna. Whether she was or wasn't pretty 'enough' was not, in the end, what her emotional well-being depended on. She could see that there were supermodels who starved themselves from a conviction of their ugliness and plain people who accepted their looks with graceful ease. Contentment had nothing to do with physique, it was an echo of an early sense of having been able to please those on whom one depended. There was nothing especially wrong with Anna's looks; the pain, such as it was, came from a family drama – and that was where her tears, intelligence and efforts at recovery would henceforth need to be directed.

In one of Anna's self-help books, she read: 'Imagine what you might wish you had done on your deathbed. Then do it now.' She could imagine certain of her more sophisticated friends flinching at the bluntness and naivety of the recommendation. But it seemed to contain everything that she most needed to hear, so much so that she would have wanted an artist to write the idea down in gigantic letters on her living room wall so that she would never again be able to forget how little time there was left to do what she really craved.

At the same time, she knew full well what she would have regretted not doing on her anticipated deathbed: resigning from her job and resuming her veterinary course. Which was why, a year after beginning with Dr Devi, she told her boss that she would be leaving in the summer and heading back to her studies the following September. She returned to the Royal Veterinary College in London and began a thesis on anticoagulant therapy in smaller mammals. She looked forward to working with horses and dogs – and one day moving to the country. On her first day back, her colleagues sent her a bouquet of flowers and an orange and polenta cake by way of thanks for what she'd done for them.

New Love

From the stalking Anna could do online, it emerged that Joachim would no longer be an option for her – not that she had continued to place huge hopes in any case. He was married to an Ecuadorian woman and living in Hamburg, with a child on the way. She looked at his posts and pictures for long enough to appreciate all that she might have missed through her carelessness and defensiveness. And she grew determined never to be so foolish with anyone again. At least it was easy to know what to do when Jake tried, repeatedly and with mounting desperation, to ask her out for dinner.

Anna signed up for profiles on a handful of dating apps and swiped with appropriate doses of hope and scepticism. Eventually, her attention was caught by Ahmed, three years older than her, an anaesthetist in a London hospital, who had kind eyes, a wry expression and a melancholic, warm smile. His photos aside, it was his brief description of himself that sealed her interest: 'Recovering crazy person. Runt of the litter. Interested in honest conversation, therapy, dancing (badly), art and a few ideas, mostly yours. Loves dogs too.'

It had been so long; she bought herself a dress especially for the occasion, though hardly dared to admit this to herself, let alone any of her girl-friends. The dress was a gentle green, with a flowery pattern. It spoke of spring, delicacy, and joy.

It was fortunate, in the circumstances, that the first thing Ahmed said when they met was: 'I hope you bought this lovely dress just for this occasion because I actually bought myself this suit – and I have the receipt to prove it.'

She made him laugh a lot, from the very beginning.

She loved that there was little subtext with Ahmed. He said pretty much whatever was on his mind – however ridiculous, touching or raw it might be – and trusted that the truth would do. He also looked particularly nice in his suit: a dark blue number that hung lightly off his angular, slender frame. Their date was at a newly opened Indian restaurant in Westbourne Grove. He explained the choice. His mother was Scottish, from Dundee, his father from Chennai. No, he had no idea where he belonged, and had long ago stopped trying to feel settled anywhere. But he knew what food he preferred, and hoped she'd not feel she had missed out on haggis.

There had, as with her, been considerable difficulties in his life. He felt comfortable opening himself up almost as soon as an implausibly large dish of Masala Dosa had been set between them. He had had a nervous breakdown three years before. The pressure on him to achieve and impress his high-ranking, plastic surgeon father had been too much. He had perhaps needed to experience what it would be like to let everyone down – and witness the liberating realisation that the world could go on. He had been in therapy three times a week ever since, with a Dr Sklar – who had apparently been the one to suggest the new suit.

Ahmed had just the right attitude to his own psychological difficulties: neither too far involved with them to slip into moroseness or folly, nor too distant from them to give off an atmosphere of denial or coldness. He exuded a sense that life was troubling for everyone and that it was best to remain honest, curious and open at all times about the challenges.

They had started sharing a delicious Gulab Jamun when Ahmed asked, with ease and charm, 'So tell me now, Anna, in what ways are *you* mad?'

And such was the setting and the warmth he had created, Anna had no hesitation in telling him pretty much the whole story.

Anna realised that what she had always wanted was an outsider: someone who didn't fit neatly into any existing social circle, who had had a miserable adolescence, who regularly asked themselves why they didn't have much in common with their friends and who disagreed with most of what was taken to be normal. But what she especially liked about Ahmed was that he wore his outsider's status without bitterness or bravado; it wasn't anyone's fault, nor was it anything to be proud of. He was just quietly on the hunt, as he put it in a text after their meal, for a fellow weirdo to spend time with.

It was a reflection of the honesty between them that at the end of the second date they were able to reveal to one another that they would eventually love to sleep together, but because it had been a long time, and both had acquired a fair number of hang-ups, they wouldn't try yet – but would look to have fun in other ways instead.

'We can imagine we're both virgins – and very shy ones at that,' said Ahmed conspiratorially.

It was among the sexiest proposals Anna had ever heard.

A lot of the fun turned out to involve dancing. Not in a club, both were far too unfashionable for that, but in her flat, and then his. They allowed themselves to be unrestrictedly silly and ecstatic, flailing their arms and legs with abandon, while playing tracks that included Lady Gaga's 'Bad Romance', Rihanna's 'We Found Love' and (this historic number became their favourite), Irene Cara's 'Flashdance'. After that, there was really nothing they ever needed to be embarrassed about again in front of one another. Sex, when it came, was the easy bit.

They became a couple who discussed sensitive topics at enormous length – long before these could become problems for them. To outsiders, it might have appeared intolerable, to Ahmed and Anna, the habit was pleasingly continuous with their respective psychotherapies. What if one of them developed a desire to sleep with someone else? How did they feel about sulking? What were their attachment patterns? Did one or both of them have daddy issues? What could they do about their likely unconscious drives to repeat masochistic childhood schemas? They enjoyed analysing their stories as much as – and perhaps even more than – they ever enjoyed living them.

Conclusion

Six months after they began seeing one another, Anna invited Ahmed to Essex to meet her parents. Anna's mother had in an earlier call told her that she had nothing whatsoever against Asian men – and, of course, didn't have a racist bone in her body – but she sincerely didn't feel someone from India would be right for her, just in terms of her eventual happiness, society being the way it was.

'That's the sort of mum I like to work my charms on,' replied Ahmed. 'Nothing better than trying to prove myself in front of a deeply disapproving audience; it's my childhood all over again.'

As it turned out, the charm offensive succeeded at the first hurdle.

'You didn't tell me he was *good looking*,' whispered Anna's mother in the kitchen.

'Oh God, Mum,' sighed Anna, 'I think we're going to need to have you locked up!'

Her father turned out to be no less complicated to bring on side. All that was required there was the discovery of a mutual interest in military history. Five minutes in and the two men were in an impassioned discussion of Winston Churchill's History of the Second World War – and it was plain sailing thereafter.

It was a sunny weekend and Anna took Ahmed to the local park where she had played as a girl. There was a man with his daughter, swinging her patiently and rather tirelessly on the swing, to the child's evident delight.

'See, it doesn't need to be so complicated,' said Ahmed, looking on at the scene.

Anna took his hand. She smiled shyly.

'A woman who worries so much that she is going to be a terrible mother is going to be a great mother,' said Ahmed, picking up a thread of a number of earlier conversations. 'Allow me to be sure of one thing for once.'

She loved this man, very much indeed.

Not every day would be easy. Anna's wounds ran deep. There were times when the earlier self-doubts returned and her esteem sagged. But she was better able to understand what was happening to her and why. She had a story to tell about who she was and where her vulnerabilities lay. She was becoming who she had always wanted to be. Anna graduated from veterinary college with one of the highest degrees in her year, and shortly after she and Ahmed moved to a small house on the outskirts of Ipswich and took up their respective professions. On the fourth anniversary of their first meeting, on a walk along the banks of the river Orwell, they agreed to begin trying for a child.

Afterword

Our societies have, for a long time, divided books into two broad categories: fiction and non-fiction. Along with this categorisation come powerful ideas about what each type of book is for. Broadly speaking, non-fiction is associated with learning and ideas; a non-fiction book is typically expected to teach us something: the history of the Second World War, the best way to start a company, or the route to interpreting the unspoken needs of a newborn child.

By contrast, the purpose of fiction is framed in a more expansive and deliberately less determinate way. Novels are associated with entertainment. It's what we read in order to relax. We may pick up a novel to be transported to another world, to lose ourselves in a story, or to develop an attachment to compelling characters with whom we can identify. Yet, in general, we might say that fiction is not connected with any particular purpose. Indeed, the word has often felt somewhat out of place in this context: why should a good novel have a purpose beyond itself? Why can it not simply rest on its merits without being asked to do anything in particular?

Since its foundation, The School of Life has published works of non-fiction, with a particular focus on psychological matters. We have discussed mental health, anxiety, calm, friendship, love, kindness and hope, among many other themes. Our aims are overtly and candidly practical. With modesty and integrity, we are interested in helping the reader (and ourselves) to cope better with the vicissitudes of life. We aim to be a thoughtful companion at some of the most challenging and confusing moments of existence: at the end of a relationship, in a period of loss, at a crossroads in a career. We hope that a reader might close one of our books feeling a little less pained and alone.

Why then have we taken the truly perplexing step of venturing into fiction? Why – of all genres – have we decided to publish a novel? The move is not as strange as it might first appear, but in order to render it less surprising, we should consider a fundamental question: what is a novel for? In our eyes, there need be no conflict between a work of fiction and a vehicle for ideas; between the pleasures associated with reading a story and the benefits typically connected with learning. A work of fiction can be a supreme educative tool, and as adept at conveying ideas as any biography or essay. Indeed, the great novels have always carried a blend of purposes: *War and Peace*, *The Pillow Book* or *Mrs Dalloway* are intrinsically far more than mere 'entertainment'; they are evidently and plainly guides to life. It is just an unfair quirk of bibliographic classification that we have come to draw such a firm line between the mission of a non-fiction work and the pleasures of a novel.

The stories of other people have a central role to play in illuminating our own narratives. A novel well used can be a telescope through which we more clearly see events in our lives that we might until now have experienced only with a painful degree of confusion or puzzlement. It may be the story of another person that best captures facets of our own trajectory; it can be in the description of someone else's feelings that we finally grasp what we have been going through for so long.

In producing a novel, The School of Life is therefore not as odd as might be imagined. We have not abandoned our earlier commitments to learning and psychological development. We have merely extended the range of tools by which we hope to fulfil our foundational aims.

Anna, the heroine of this novel, is distinctly her own person. She is as 'real' a character as any in a work of fiction, with fine-grained and individual characteristics and a particular way of looking at the world and her journey through it. At the same time, she is a part of all of us, and someone from whose experiences we might pick up ideas that can be applied to situations far beyond those in the novel.

Too often, we face an uncomfortable dichotomy in a bookshop: between non-fiction that is seen as good for us but perhaps slightly hard work, and fiction that is deemed fun but perhaps lacking in educational intent. We hope to return the novel to a more interesting and more rewarding mission: that of entertaining *and* teaching us; of delighting *and* instructing us.

Also available from The School of Life:

A Job to Love

How to find a fulfilling career

A practical guide to finding fulfilling work by understanding yourself.

Alongside a satisfying relationship, a career we love is one of the most important requirements for a fulfilled life. Unfortunately, it is devilishly hard to understand oneself well enough to know quite where one's energies should be directed.

It is to help us out of some of these impasses that we wrote *A Job to Love,* a guide to how we can better understand ourselves and locate a job that is right for us. With compassion and a deeply practical spirit, the book guides us to discover our true talents and to make sense of our confused desires and aspirations before it is too late.

UK ISBN: 978-1-915087-06-5
US ISBN: 978-1-915087-31-7

THE SCHOOL OF LIFE

RELATIONSHIPS

Learning to love

Relationships

Learning to love

A book to inspire closeness and connection, helping people not only to find love but to make it last.

Few things promise us greater happiness than our relationships – yet few things more reliably deliver misery and frustration. Our error is to suppose that we are born knowing how to love and that managing a relationship might therefore be intuitive and easy.

This book starts from a different premise: that love is a skill to be learnt, rather than just an emotion to be felt. It calmly and charmingly takes us around the key issues of relationships, from arguments to sex, forgiveness to communication, making sure that success in love need never again be just a matter of luck.

UK ISBN: 978-1-912891-97-9
US ISBN: 978-1-915087-13-3

Stay or Leave

How to remain in, or end, your relationship

A book to offer clarity and guidance when facing the difficult decision of whether your relationship has a future.

Whether we should stay in or leave a relationship is one of the most consequential and painful decisions we are ever likely to confront. What makes the issue so hard is that there are no fixed rules for judgement. How can we tell whether a relationship is 'good enough' or plain wrong? How do we draw the line between justified longing and naivety? Does someone 'better' actually exist?

All these questions typically haunt our minds as we weigh up whether to stay or go. *Stay or Leave* walks us gently through our options, opening our minds to perspectives we might not have considered.

This book aims to take the reader towards a time, presently hard to imagine, when the choice will no longer feel so agonising. Using its lessons, we can understand ourselves deeply, consider our options, minimise our regrets and find the way ahead.

ISBN: 978-1-912891-40-5

Also available from The School of Life:

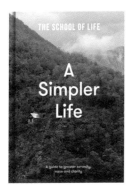

A Simpler Life

A guide to greater serenity, ease and clarity

Exploring ideas around minimalism, simplicity and how to live comfortably with less.

The modern world can be a complicated and noisy place, filled with too many options, products and ideas. That explains why what many of us long for is simplicity: a life that can be more pared down, peaceful and focused on the essentials.

But finding simplicity is not always easy; it isn't just a case of emptying out our closets or trimming back commitments in our diaries. True simplicity requires that we understand the roots of our distractions – and develop a canny respect for the stubborn reasons why things can grow complex and overwhelming.

This book is a guide to the simpler lives we crave and deserve. It takes a psychological approach, considering how we might achieve simplicity across a range of areas: our relationships, social lives, work routines and our approaches to possessions and media. We have for too long been drowning in excess and clutter from a confusion about our aspirations; *A Simpler Life* helps us tune out the static and focus on what properly matters to us.

ISBN: 978-1-912891-68-9

To join The School of Life community and find out more, scan below:

The School of Life publishes a range of books on essential topics in psychological and emotional life, including relationships, parenting, friendship, careers and fulfilment. The aim is always to help us to understand ourselves better and thereby to grow calmer, less confused and more purposeful. Discover our full range of titles, including books for children, here:

www.theschooloflife.com/books

The School of Life also offers a comprehensive therapy service, which complements, and draws upon, our published works:

www.theschooloflife.com/therapy